Humor is No Laughing Matter
ISBN 0-9730780-4-9

Copyright © 2006 by Ross Mackay

Printed and Bound in Canada
Fourth Printing

Edited by Anne Toner Fung
Illustrations by Laura Parkin
Cover design by Clulow & Associates

No part of this book may be reproduced in any form by any electronic or mechanical means without permission in writing from the publisher, other than for brief passages used for reviewing purposes.

Ross Mackay

Humor is No Laughing Matter

Many speakers don't use humor because they feel thay can't tell a joke. This is rarely true, and this book will reveal a very practical side to the use of humor which allows most people to create more fun for their audiences.

By sharing a laugh with business associates, it becomes much easier to share a problem with them, and also arrive at the solution.

When there is love and laughter in the home, the world is a better place, and the happiness and humor will sustain us throughout our lives.

This book is dedicated to helping you get more joy out of living by providing a tonic for your speeches, your work and your life.

Ross Mackay
Aurora, Ontario
July, 2006

Contents

Why Humor	1
The Ingredients	7
Humor at Home	23
Humor in the Workplace	27
Humor on the Platform	41
Seven Rules of Humor on the Platform	59
Cultivating Your Own Sense of Humor	77
Conclusion	94

Why Humor?

It's funny, but I've been waiting a long time for this to happen... something that I enjoy is now good for me! In fact, it turns out that it's always been good for me. Although I've always considered humor as simply good fun, over the last couple of decades it has proved so beneficial for all of us, that even the medical profession is beginning to recognize and applaud the therapeutic effects of a gigantic guffaw or even a good giggle.

A visit to my family doctor usually subjects me to his 'unique' brand of humor. While it rarely elicits a rollicking knee-slapper type of response, his ever present jokes always relieve at least a portion of whatever tension I may be experiencing. A significant percentage of his patients walk out of his office much happier, and feeling much better about themselves, than they were when they entered... regardless of their medical condition.

A resounding belly laugh has been shown to reduce blood pressure to a point even slightly below the normal relaxation rate. Any laughter will exercise the lungs and raise the level of oxygen in the blood. In addition, it has been proved that 20 minutes of laughter will burn the same number of calories as 20 minutes of jogging!

O.K., so I fabricated the last one, but I wanted to make sure I still had your attention, because it is true that laughter stimulates many of the same positive physiological changes as exercise.

Regular and frequent measures of merriment will create enough fun in everyone's life to raise the joy level of situations and alleviate our stress levels. And it's worth remembering that stress has been identified as one of the major causes of illness and death in today's society.

"It is also known that death is nature's way of telling us to slow down."

Other studies have revealed that a joyous outlook encourages expansive thinking and improves our ability to solve problems; a major reason to encourage laughter in the business world. Sadly too many traditional thinkers in the ranks of senior corporate management still believe that laughter in the workplace is an interrupting influence and downright counter-productive.

More enlightened executives recognize that water-cooler mirth is liable to create happier and healthier employees in a more relaxed and enjoyable workplace. All of which will translate into reduced absenteeism, increased staff retention, higher productivity and greater profit levels.

One of the biggest advantages of maintaining a humorous attitude is that it provides us with a powerful sense of perspective and balance in our lives. Not only does it allow us to flourish in a hectic environment (currently referred to as 'pursuing a career' or 'having a life'), it also helps us build relationships with others much more quickly, and maintain those relationships far more easily.

So why don't we have more fun in our lives? This question becomes even more relevant when we understand that, as children, we laugh over 400 times every day, yet, by the time we reach the age of 35, that frequency has plummeted to 15.

Why...? Simple. We grew up. We matured. We started a career, and *everyone knows* that you've got to get serious eventually. So we got serious and we became busy. Ask 10 of your friends today, "How are you doing?" At least 8 of them will tell you, "I'm busy, I'm soooo busy, I'm working all the hours God sends and a few he doesn't even know about."

O.K. so maybe most of them won't have the sense of humor to use that last line, but the reality is that we're all so busy making a living, we forget about living a life.

I fell into the same trap when I was in my early 30's. I was so busy that I eventually received the age-old award of the busy... an Ulcer! And this was before the days of the palm pilot and cell phone.

From that experience, let me give you some advice... GET OVER IT! Start laughing again, release the joy inside you and focus on having fun. To quote a favourite phrase of professional speaker and consultant, Linda Tarrant, CSP,

> "Life is too short to be miserable".

You know you need some humor in your life when.....

"..... your idea of a joke
is that someone else is sent
to that conference in Kalamazoo."

"..... you know someone's a visitor to your office
because she's smiling."

"..... working only half a day means
you can do what you like
with the other 12 hours."

Don't worry, be happy. That musical advice from an earlier era, gives us the secret of a more joyful and more productive existence. When we're happy, we're much more relaxed and that is the condition in which we can access our optimum performance capabilities.

Olympic sprinters who are preparing to launch their bodies over 100 metres in less than 10 seconds don't prepare by tensing their muscles and their minds. On the contrary, they spend the last few seconds before coming under starter's orders, jumping up and down and shaking their arms and legs to release the tension and increase relaxation.

Actors and professional speakers regularly employ various relaxation techniques in preparation for their entrance or introduction.

CEO's can be found practising Yoga or receiving a shoulder massage in the middle of the work day to reduce tension and increase relaxation in order to achieve this optimum performance level. It also helps them avoid the trap (some call it the death trap) of becoming too intensely entangled in their work.

Now I'm not suggesting we should sit around half the day with our feet on the desk and our brains in neutral, but the old adage that it's better to work smart, not hard, still applies. And part of working smart involves developing a humorous outlook that better prepares you to survive the tension and stress that can be part of so many careers.

The Ingredients

Every type of humor has the same ingredients which naturally evolve from a view of humor that states;

"Humor takes place when a thought or action unexpectedly disrupts the mind's logical process."

Naturally, this first assumes that our mind has a "logical thought process". If not we must first create one. This is called the *"Set-up".*

We then disrupt that process in a manner that we hope will be surprising and humorous. That is called the *"Punch-line".*

Every humour format has these two parts. The biggest difference is in the nature and quality of the Set-up, and that will depend on the format used. The more misdirection that is created by the Set-up, the greater the surprise will be when the Punch-line is delivered. It is that element of surprise that is supposed to create the humor.

The young couple were at the drive-in when the girl said, "I would feel so much more romantic if we could just look up at the stars above us."
At which point the young man immediately set about taking the top down. He later bragged about it to his friends, telling them, "I had that top down in less than 10 minutes".

"That's ridiculous!" said his friend,
"I can get mine down in 15 seconds".

"Maybe so", said the young man,
"but you've got a convertible!!".

This joke is particularly effective because of two conditions:
1. The punchline is completely surprising, and
2. The 'Punchword' is the last word spoken.

The Pun:

This play on words depends on ambiguity and innuendo for it's humorous result. In spite of the skilled knowledge and use of the English language that is essential for it's purposeful usage, it is generally looked down on as somewhat inferior. Oscar Wilde was reputed to have said,
>"The pun is the lowest form of wit....
>....unless you thought of it first."

> e.g. "It's better to have loved a short girl than never to have loved at all."

> e.g. "My grandfather lived until he was 93 years old and never used glasses. He drank straight from the bottle."

When the Pun is used, the most frequent response is usually a groan from the audience. In view of this, most professional speech writers will not use it.

For the Pun to be a positive influence in any presentation, it requires that a degree of trust has already been established between the speaker and the audience. Under such circumstances, the Pun is still likely to elicit a groan response, but this time, it will be based on a shared enjoyment of the joke. Also, the groan is frequently a tacit acknowledgement of the skill required to create the pun in the first place.

The out-dated Shaggy Dog Story usually had an extremely long and involved (and usually ludicrous) Set-up, with a Pun as the Punch-line. Owing to it's length, this format was rarely used as a portion of any kind of presentation and consequently has dropped out of common usage. The level of humor involved usually depended on the skill of the story-teller, as the set-up would frequently last as long as 10 – 15 mins. before the punch-line was reached.

The One-Liner:

This format is another type of abbreviated joke. It depends on a very succinct Set-up, or one that has already been established by reputation.

e.g. "Talk about being cheap! Yesterday my Husband was so short of money, he had to draw some out of his bank account."

In this example, the Set-up is very brief.... "Talk about being cheap! my husband....". However, it can also work if you're talking about a specific individual and you already know they have a reputation of being frighteningly frugal.

For those of you who don't get out much, you should know that we Scotsmen have such a reputation (It is totally unfounded and unfair, but it still persists.) Therefore, if we're discussing a Scotsman, we could change the already brief Set-up to one word, "He".

"He was so short of money, he had to draw some out of his bank account."

A good rule of thumb to note at this point is that it is usually unwise to tell a joke at the expense of a group to which you do not belong. More on this later.

In his nightly monologue on the old "Tonight Show", host and comedian Johnnie Carson, developed a particular style of One-liner that used exaggeration together with a simple but effective audience involvement.

> e.g. "My neighbourhood was soooo tough."
> (response) "How tough was it?"
> "Any cat with a tail was a tourist."

> e.g. "My sister is soooo Tall."
> (response) "How tall is she?"
> "She can hunt geese with a rake."

The major benefit of a One-liner is that it can be fitted into a presentation without a major disruption in the flow of material. It can be used very effectively to lighten up a moment in an otherwise heavy topic without actually interrupting the point being made.

>   *e.g.* "My husband is soooo Dumb."
>   (response) "How dumb is he?"
>   "He thinks Boys II Men is a day care centre."

In such circumstances it can be delivered as a casual "throw-away" line, or it can be expressed with some emphasis to underscore a point.

Humor is No Laughing Matter

The Standard Joke:

This format is the same as for the One-liner, except that the Set-up is usually quite a bit longer.

> *"When my brother hit 40 years of age,*
> *he had to get bifocals,*
> *This has made it extremely difficult for him*
> *to keep up with the news.*
> *He can now only read*
> *the bottom half of the newspaper."*

In many instances, the Set-up can become a fairly lengthy tale. The danger of a long Set-up is that the Punch-line must be worth waiting for.

One way of overcoming the problem of a lengthy Set-up is to ensure that it serves more than one Punch-line.

> *The Vet was annoyed at going bald at an early age, but he noticed that dogs never lose their hair. He therefore injected himself with some hormones from an Irish Setter..... It worked beautifully.........*

- *Of course his ears kept falling in his food!*

   - *And his wife wouldn't let him up on the couch!*

   - *Because he had fleas!*

This is an extremely brief and very obvious example, but frequently the multiple laugh lines can be spaced throughout a story and culminate with the major punch-line. This is where the story-telling art comes into play. A very short joke can often be developed into a longer story with many laughs and involve the reinforcement of an important point in the lesson being delivered.

The Vignette:

This is usually a short story involving a moral or lesson. The popular series of books, "Chicken Soup for the Soul" by Jack Canfield and Mark Victor Hansen employs collections of such stories.

This style is frequently used by many Professional Speakers who draw from their personal experience to emphasise the point of their message. They are frequently referred to as their "Signature Stories".

When humorous, the use of these stories must invoke the same warning as the long joke. The Punchline must be worth waiting for.

Another way of using the humorous Vignette, is to sprinkle a series of One-liners throughout it. A great story-teller like Grady Jim Robinson never keeps you waiting any significant length of time for a laugh. Although his stories always have an intellectual point, and always have a major laugh at the end, the entire story will be a series of funny events or situations that help build the story to a humorous climax.

Comedian or Clown

As individuals, we are subjected to many different types of humor. They vary from the Comedian to the Clown. The popular Comedians of today perform in comedy clubs where children or others of a more sensitive nature are rarely found. The type of comedy typically expounded in these arenas consists of a verbal barrage of robust jokes or one-liners which are solely focused on making people laugh.

The Clown has a different appeal. He or she uses various forms of "slap-stick" comedy, all of which involve considerable use of body language. The masters of this type of comedy throughout the 20th century included people like Charlie Chaplin, Red Skelton, Jerry Lewis, Lucille Ball and Dick Van Dyke, all of whom were capable of eliciting a wide range of emotions from their audiences. However, they are particularly remembered for their efforts in getting themselves in and out of difficult and amusing situations.

Both Comedians and Clowns evolved from the Court Jester of the Middle Ages. In mediaeval England, every family of the nobility, and particularly the Royal Court, had a Jester, or a Fool. While their principle function was to entertain, it extended far beyond that. They also had to ease any tension that may arise during Court business. They alone could poke fun at the King, but sometimes even they went too far and had to bail themselves out of trouble with their quick wit.

> In a moment of fury on one such occasion, the King ordered that the Fool be executed. Shortly thereafter, the King realised he had been too hasty. However, the King's word was law and, as he had given his word, the sentence must be carried out. As a gesture of remorse, the King told the Fool, "As I have commanded it, you must die. But, in recognition of your service to this Court over the years, you may choose the manner of your own death." To which the Fool replied, "in that case your Majesty, I choose to die of old age."

That example of quick-wittedness removed the tension from the situation and allowed the Monarch to keep his word while extricating himself from a self-imposed awkward position. In addition, it helped him maintain his important image as the supreme authority in the land. This is a powerful example of how we can use humor to defuse a difficult situation at home, in the office, or on the platform.

The difference between the extremes of Comedian and Clown today usually lies in the amount of thought the audience has to exercise in order to "get" the joke.

We've all laughed at the Clown who slipped on a banana peel and finished up on their back looking foolish. Minimal thought process was involved other than the self-reassurance that "they're O.K., they didn't really get hurt...".

Although we all know that laughing at the misfortunes of others is inappropriate, it can be rendered acceptable if we realise that it is being set up by the Clown with the express purpose of having you laugh at the Clown. In other words, it becomes a self directed simple type of humor which offends no-one and requires almost no thought at all.

Compare that with the more intellectual humor you may hear on some comedic TV sitcoms or talk shows, and those such as "Whose Line Is It Anyway?". In this show, the comedians are given a ludicrous word, topic or situation with which to create a scene, with hilarious results.

Comedian and television Talk Show Host, David Letterman has become famous for his "Top Ten Lists" where he takes a wide variety of topical issues and situations and pokes fun at them in the same way. The repetition of his television show and the presentation of the Top Ten Lists, has also created that degree of anticipation that is so helpful for an effective punch line.

Here is an example of a Top Ten List of the Shortest Books in the World

    10. "Human Rights in China"

    9. "The Wild Years", by Al Gore

    8. "My Plan to Find the Real Killers" by O.J. Simpson

7. "Popular Lawyers"
6. "Dr. Kevorkian's Best Motivational Speeches"
5. The Amish Phone Book.
4. "A Guide to Arab Democracies"
3. "Everything Men Know About Women"
2. "The Engineers Guide to Fashion"
1. "The Book of Virtues" by Bill Clinton

The only objective of a Comedian is to get the audience to laugh. Some may also use their humor to encourage you to think about a particular topic. For example, many Comedians will use their comedic talent to have you reconsider a political incident or individual as in the example given above. However, their main objective is to make you laugh. To accomplish this they will frequently resort to topics and language that would be inappropriate in any other setting.

The Trainer or Speaker however, is on the platform to make a point, teach a lesson, or bring you a message. They use humor to underscore and to illuminate these points.

As a result of this, both the type of humor and it's format will be very important to the individual's performance and effectiveness.

The same will apply to a corporate setting where the type of humor used and it's format will also be very important, and quite different from a Clown or a Comedian.

Humor at Home

By the time my two daughters had reached their teen years, they clearly understood that their father's main goal in life was to embarrass them in public.

Every parent laughs and plays with their children to some extent. But frequently, we don't extend that same sense of fun to our other relatives or even our spouses. As a youngster, I well remember times when my father would have his mother-in-law laughing so hard that her face and sides hurt, and she could hardly move from the enjoyment. Frequently, I didn't understand what Grandma found funny, but it didn't matter. All that mattered was that the laughter and joy pouring out of her became infectious and everyone started to laugh, including me, in spite of the fact that I didn't "get" the joke. I laughed because everyone else was laughing. Laughter is infectious.

When there is love and laughter in a home, the whole world is a better place. How do you feel when a child looks up at you and smiles? When I walk through the door to my daughter's home, my Grandsons look up at me with huge grins on their faces, and I immediately become a kid again. They smile the way every child smiles. It starts deep down in that place my friend and author, Anne Toner Fung, calls, "the giggle centre of your soul", and then travels up to shine out of the eyes.

Humor and happiness start at home and carry us safely through the rest of our lives. When I was only 16 years old, Dad passed away. I had three other siblings, with the baby being only a few months old. To say that the ensuing few years were difficult for my mother would be a gross under-statement. There were few government agencies to help a single mother in those days. She had to rely on her job as an auxiliary nurse, working night shift 4 nights a week, and the generosity of friends and family.

Not only did we survive, but it's a tribute to her courage and positive outlook, that one of my most prominent memories of these difficult times was what we called our 'family song', which included the

important (to us) line......
"Not much money, oh but honey, ain't we got fun."

Laughter and happiness can help overcome a lot of minor family squabbles and a whole bunch of the big ones too. While I enjoyed Richard Carlson's book, "Don't Sweat the Small Stuff", and applaud it's concept, I had difficulty accepting the sub-title "...And It's All Small Stuff". The reality is that many people have to face some "Big Stuff" in their lives, and the appropriate use of humor will always help them get through it. At a later time, I was delighted to find a copy of one of his subsequent books entitled,
"What About the Big Stuff".

Many of us have attended the funeral of a loved one and, while we were reminiscing about them with others during the reception, found ourselves laughing and smiling about the things the deceased had enjoyed throughout his or her life. In spite of the tradition that we're not supposed to laugh at funerals for fear of hurting someone else's feeling, sometimes humor is appropriate.

Lillian went through her life with a wonderful sense of fun. There was nothing she enjoyed more than a good joke (even the risque ones!). When I delivered the eulogy at her funeral, I read out a number of jokes she had listed on a piece of paper we found in her purse. It was a fitting part of the funeral service for a jovial and fun-loving lady. It also served to notify everyone in attendance that her family would be not be upset to hear laughter during that trying time.

Humor in the Workplace

Humor in the workplace is still considered by many to be an interrupting influence and frequently counter-productive.

According to this line of thinking, when you display any joyful tendencies, you distract yourself and others from work, and reduce corporate productivity.

This dismal attitude evolved during the days of industrial drudgery, and was still prevalent into the second half of the 20th century. Although it continues in many areas today, the reasons now tend to be the contemporary results of hectic schedules and demanding workloads.

It is obvious that excessive clowning and tomfoolery can reduce your efficiency and output as well as disturbing those around you. However, the opposite extreme reveals the more serious problem of people who take themselves far too seriously, and who have forgotten how to have fun.

Ask yourself some questions.....

When was the last time I laughed in the office without feeling guilty?

When was the last time I looked forward going to the office in the morning?

When was the last time I felt happy and proud about finishing a project?

When was the last time my boss told me a funny joke?

When was the last time I told my boss a joke?

An article in a recent edition of a leading business magazine identified that one of the 10 most important attributes of a successful boss was a sense of humour. The interesting part was that this attribute only appeared on the list created by the employees. It did not show up on the 10 most important attributes that the bosses felt were important.

Five Reasons for More Humor at Work

1. *It creates a fun place to work.*

The TGIF attitude (thank goodness it's Friday) is all too prevalent in business today. Many come to work just to fill in time between weekends. In the book "Fish" by Stephen Lundin, Harry Paul and John Christensen, we are taught that even the most mundane tasks can be made easier to bear if the work environment is enjoyable. The concept of their book is.....
"Work Made Fun, Get's Done".

In a fun atmosphere people realise they are valued individuals and as employees, they therefore tend to stay with the company much longer and take fewer sick days.

Recently, I was invited to speak to a sales group in a market that was highly competitive. When I asked the manager what she wanted me to achieve with my talk, she found it difficult to identify anything specific other than "just motivate them a bit".

In exploring this a bit deeper I asked why they needed motivating, she said, "Well, everyone needs a bit of a boost now and again." Further questions revealed that she did not want me to include any sales techniques in the presentation as she felt that they were already well trained.

It turned out that the Sales Manager was simply trying to give her staff an interesting and enjoyable diversion combined with a little motivation. I also learned that minimum length of service in this 30+ strong sales team in this difficult market was in excess of 5 years. This was a group of sales people who were working in a happy environment where they were made to feel special on a regular basis and consequently stayed with that company.

2. It creates a healthier environment.

Nothing is quite so devastating to the health of a company's work force than the debilitating effect of stress. It inhibits logical thought and conceptual thinking, it reduces efficiency, and it increases sickness and absenteeism.

All the stress management programs available to people today, involve the ability to relax in one form or another. It should come as no surprise to learn that one of the most effective ways to relax is by laughing. Evidence of this is found in the enormous success of the use of humor in the series of Corporate Training Videos recorded by John Cleese of Monty Python fame.

In addition to it's ability to help you relax, humor has been recognized for it's curative properties. Many people are familiar with the story of Norman Cousins from his book, "The Anatomy of an Illness". Cousins had been diagnosed as terminally ill and hospitalized with a debilitating disease of the nervous system. He determined that he would never get well in a place full of sick people, and checked himself out. When his doctor argued, he gave in to the extent that he checked himself into a hotel across the street. He then had friends bring him video tapes of the Three Stooges, the Marx Brothers, Lewis and Martin, etc. which he viewed all the time. His pain was so great he could not sleep. Laughing for 10 solid minutes, he found, relieved the pain for several hours so he could sleep. He fully recovered from his illness and lived another 20 happy, healthy and productive years, and he credits visualization and laughter for his recovery.

Some people think laughter is a waste of time. It is a luxury, they say, a frivolity, something to indulge in only every so often. Norman Cousins believed that the body's natural painkillers, endorphins, are produced when we laugh. Other studies are progressing that suggest additional cells that are an important part of your immune system are released in even greater numbers during times of laughter.

In his book, "Managing to Have Fun", Matt Weinstein points out;
> "You don't play when you feel better,
> you feel better when you play."

3. It develops camaraderie.

The company that laughs together, stays together. The same is true for the departments within a company. You can't laugh with someone you don't like or with whom you're fighting. So keep laughing and enjoy each other's company.

> *The new golfer said,*
> *"I'd move heaven and earth to break 100."*
> *his partner said, "Concentrate on heaven,*
> *you've already moved enough earth."*

Many companies have bowling leagues, or golf outings, or theatre groups, or even softball and/or hockey teams that play against other companies. These activities are not work related..... or are they? They bring together all the participants so that they can get to know each other on a personal level which gives them the licence to have fun with each other, and laugh together.

The team spirit that is created transmits itself into the workplace and brings everyone together for the common goals of profitability and job security.

Some years ago I worked in a company where all the golfers played together after work on a Thursday evening. As this was in the Toronto area in Canada, there were only a couple of months in the year when we could actually complete the full 18 holes. Early and late in the season we would simply golf until we couldn't see the ball or the green anymore.

> *Why are you so late for your tee-off time?*
> *It's Sunday, I had to toss a coin*
> *to decide between Church and Golf.*
> *But why are you so late?*
> *I had to toss the coin 23 times.*

In addition to the enjoyment of the game and the individual competition (and the fact that you really get to know someone's character when you play golf with them!), we found that a number of business problems were solved in the relaxed atmosphere of the golf course.

Two of the most avid golfers in that group were the Shop Labourer and the Plant Manager who rarely had a chance to interact with each other during the course of the workday, but who enjoyed each other's company on the golf course.

4. It improves communication.

When you can share a laugh with an associate who works with you or in another department, it becomes much easier to share a problem with them. It also facilitates the solution. People who have fun with each other not only enjoy each other's company but will trust each other more when it comes to expressing their business views.

This makes it easier for us to share our feelings, our beliefs and our concerns. As a result of increased trust, we will be more open with our comments and the extent to which we consider the other person's point of view.

> "My daughter and I have one thing in common.
> She listens to Rock Groups
> and I listen to Economists.
> Neither one of us
> understands a word they're saying."

Communication is so much more than simply talking at or to each other. We have to seek to understand what other people are saying. This can be particularly challenging in a group of people trying to share ideas or solve a problem.

> "My wife and I communicate very well,
> We both understand that I make
> all the important decisions in this marriage,
> and she decides whether or not we'll act on them."

When you are part of a group discussion or a meeting where the tension is starting to rise, look for ways to say or do something funny which will create a laugh and relieve that tension. Be careful not to take the topic under discussion too far away from the point, and be quick to bring it back on focus as soon as the humor has been enjoyed. This way, there is less chance of anyone considering it intrusive and time-wasting.

5. It develops a more creative and productive environment.

The basis of a more creative and productive environment is, once again, the trust that is developed between people who can have fun with each other and therefore enjoy each other's company.

When you can laugh with others in a group, it makes it easier for all members of that group to bring forth their ideas on any particular topic. This creates a wonderful atmosphere for brainstorming, where random ideas are expressed without fear of ridicule or criticism regardless of how crazy or illogical they may appear at first glance.

Can you imagine the atmosphere in the board room where someone first came up with the crazy idea that they produce a new line of computers with transparent cases in shocking pink, glaring green and brilliant blue? Wonderful!

Many of you older folks will remember the Dick Tracy comic strip in which so many "ludicrous" suggestions were introduced.

One of the most frequently used was a two-way radio in the wrist-watch. That idea must have caused a chuckle somewhere in the early discussions, after all, such a thing was impossible. Yet today we can call each other on cell phones and discuss that reality.

I wonder how many straight-laced, sober-sided corporate executives did it take to decide to change a grocery store from one where the customers stood on one side and were brought the items they wanted by a clerk behind the counter, to that of the self-serve grocery stores? Or was there a giggle or two in that meeting?

And how many people laughed at the suggestion to put a coffee shop in a book store when that was first launched. Ridiculous! Customers will spend too much time reading the books over coffee...!!!!! Wait a minute though, the longer they spend over the books, the more books they'll buy.

Aha!!! That's the kind of epiphany that can change an industry, if not indeed a whole way of life.

It all starts with the ability to work and share ideas

with others in an open and free manner, all of which is made easier when you can laugh with each other.

> *My husband is a do-it-yourself man.*
> *Every time I ask him to do something,*
> *he says, "Do it yourself!"*

One word of warning about humor in the workplace. There are some people who still believe that it is out of place, disruptive and counter-productive, and there is always a danger that it can be taken to an unacceptable extreme.

Some years ago, I worked in a small office in a building in which a number of other similarly sized businesses were located. As most people kept their door open, we quickly got to know many of the other people in the building. This facilitated our hiring a lady from one of the other offices to fill a secretarial position in our company. Within a few weeks of having started with us she approached me and told me she owed me an apology. Being somewhat mystified, I asked her why. She said, "During the time I worked down the hall, I would frequently see you passing up and down laughing and joking with everyone and I didn't think you took your work seriously, and I wasn't sure I could work in such an environment."

What a sad commentary from a young woman! She wasn't sure she could work in a place where there was a lot of fun! Later, I asked her how she felt now we had worked together for a few weeks and she said, "Oh now I realise that the only thing you don't take seriously is yourself."

When you use humor at work, make sure that your associates and your boss understand what you're doing and why. No-one likes someone who goofs off on the the job, but everyone likes someone with a sense of humor. There is a fine line between the two and it's different in every location and with every person. Beware of crossing it in your workplace.

Humor on the Platform

When was the last time you sat through a presentation or seminar and, at the end of it, walked out muttering about how terrible it was because you laughed too much? I'd be prepared to bet that it hasn't happened to any of us, but let's check out the opposite condition. How many of us have walked out at the end of a seminar muttering about how dry and boring the topic was, and how difficult it was to stay awake?

I would expect that your responses to these questions would convince you that the use of humor on the platform is essential, regardless of your topic. There are few subjects more guaranteed to send people to sleep than "Pumping Reliability in the Engineering Field", and yet that was one of my topics as a speaker and trainer.

One of the most heartfelt comments I received at the end of a particular two day session on that topic was,
>"I didn't even **want** to fall asleep!".

Although it's a dull topic which is usually delivered to a group that either thinks they know it all already, or are predisposed to be bored for the duration, I make it my business to make it fun. Why? Because I've got to live through it too, and I don't want to bore myself!

Alan was a Chemistry Professor at a major Canadian University. According to him, his job was to provide the students with the information. Whether or not they showed up to class, stayed awake to hear it, or even understood it, was not his problem. His job was to put the information in front of them. Their job was to learn and understand it.

Anyone who understands communication however, realises that the function of the speaker is to create understanding, while the job of the listener is to acknowledge and confirm understanding.

The founder of Toastmasters International, Dr. Ralph Smedley has been quoted as saying that;

"we learn better when we're in a relaxed and enjoyable frame of mind",

and nothing does that more effectively than a good joke. Toastmasters International devotes two of their Advanced Communication Programs to the use of humor. "The Entertaining Speaker" speaker manual includes valuable information on how to make an audience laugh, while the "Humorously Speaking" manual provides details on how to use stories and jokes to grab and keep listeners attention and illustrate important points.

The appropriate use of humor in presentations will improve the effectiveness of the communication process on a number of fronts.

- Humor makes the audience ready to hear the speaker.
- Humor helps the audience remember the speaker.
- Humor helps the audience remember the points for discussion.

The most effective kind of humor for use on the platform is the One-liner as it can be added to a speech without a major disruption in the flow of material. It can help make a point when used with some emphasis, or it can create a light moment as a "throw-away" line when delivered casually.

However, the longer story (vignette) which can be used to evoke as much tragedy as it does humor, can do both by the judicious use of humorous one-liners to change the tone and tempo of the story. Here lies the secret of the true value of humor in every presenters arsenal.

Frequently, we are called on to deliver a serious message, yet we are so caught up in the tragic aspect of the situation, we forget that, when we are on the platform, we are the Managers of Mirth, the Directors of Devilment, the Crown Princes of Comedy. It is our responsibility to bring out the humour and change the state of mind of the audience.

Connecting with the Audience

Until a speaker connects with an audience, he or she is simply lecturing them. By using some form of humor early in the presentation, the "Connection" process begins.

If the humor used can be self directed to the extent that it portrays the speaker's humanity and personality, then the audience starts to accept that, while that speaker may be serious about their topic, they're not necessarily going to take themselves too seriously.

This can be achieved during the opening remarks, by the introduction, or even in the manner the speaker walks onto the stage. Some years ago, David Brooks, won Toastmasters International Speech Contest the year that he walked out onto the stage wearing a tuxedo jacket and a pair of blue jeans. The audience immediately understood that there was likely to be some humor in this presentation, and they prepared themselves to listen, to hear, and to understand what was to follow. That connection was made before the speaker even opened his mouth.

Notice the difference between that and the Corporate Speaker who is going to deliver a message to a meeting of employees or shareholders, and to whom it has been suggested that they throw a few jokes in to make it light. Most of the time, these jokes have no relevance to the topic, the audience, the event, the location, or even the speaker himself and therefore don't work in that context.

Ideally the opening humor should relate to the introduction, where you are, why you're there, who the audience is and why they're there. In fact the opening humor can be contained in the introduction itself.

For this reason, Professional Speakers will rarely depend on someone else to create an introduction for them. Most will write their own introduction and request that the Master of Ceremonies read it verbatim. This allows the speaker to set up his or her presentation in the body of the introduction and create the desired atmosphere for the opening of the speech.

Of course, it is not essential that either the

introduction or the opening remarks utilise humor. This will depend on the nature of the presentation and the event. Humor should be used only when it is appropriate. But when it is the right thing to do, it will help the speaker connect with the audience and create a bond which will help the speaker and his or her topic be better accepted.

Be Memorable

Being memorable doesn't need to rely on humor at all. However, few speakers (amateur or professional) have the ability to hold an audiences attention and have them remember them and the lessons they wish to impart with the same kind of impact that can be achieved with the use of humor.

Any speaker who simply regurgitates a "Laundry List" of ideas or rules to follow, will find that very few of their audience members will be able to quote more than a couple of points on the following day. If, on the other hand, every point is reinforced by a humorous story, the retention of the ideas will increase dramatically.

The use of humor should be carefully controlled to determine how you as a speaker, and your message, will be remembered. In other words, do you simply want to be remembered as "being funny", or do you want to be remembered for the lessons imparted during your presentation?

In fact, it is particularly important not to overdo the

use of humor unless the main objective of the presentation is to entertain. Under these conditions, you are accomplishing what the meeting planner wants you to do, and you will therefore be asked back at some future date.

If however, you have been asked to impart some meaningful leadership knowledge to a team of executives, and all you do is get them laughing, then you have failed in your objective, and are unlikely to be invited to speak to that group again.

On of the most memorable presentations I have witnessed in recent years was one that relied heavily on Photographs, yet every one of them supported the single message being given. The same can be said for using humor; use as much as you like, as long as it supports and promotes your message.

Change the Pace or Tone

The concept of taking your audience on an emotional roller coaster ride has long been used in the ranks of professional speakers. This involves interspersing the "heavy" or serious passages with "lighter" or humorous ones.

As an example, it's been said that Zig Ziglar, the famous Sales and Motivational Speaker, builds in a humorous moment every 11 minutes. Many speakers will do it much more frequently, while others don't do it nearly as often. This is simply a matter of personal style and none of them is either right or wrong.

In between the Highs and Lows of the speech, are the points at which the main points are positioned for major effect.

In one of the presentations I did many years ago, I talked about the courage my mother displayed when she was widowed and had to raise 4 children single-handedly. I told how she protected us against the pain in her heart at losing the man she loved. This is a very emotional moment for the audience that creates considerable tension. Therefore, before moving on to another segment of the speech, I had to release that tension. I achieved that by singing a few lines from a song we referred to as "our family song", "... not much money, oh, but honey, ain't we got fun". I accompanied my singing with a few amateurish dance steps, following which I delivered the line,

"You see, courage can conquer talent!".

By staying with the story line and poking a little fun at myself, the tension is relieved and a fun moment is created. It is also achieved without interrupting the story line or the flow of the presentation. This allowed me a smooth transition to the next segment of the speech.

As an aside, a speaker should not include an emotional personal story if he or she is still unable to relate it without becoming overly emotional.

Make the Message More Palatable

The plight of farmers in North America has been well documented in recent years and yet, within that community you will find many examples of how humor is used to highlight the problem for certain audiences.

> *A clerk in the hardware store in the farming community became intrigued when a Farmer George started to come in every week to buy 6 hammers. When he asked him for an explanation, George told him that he was selling them to his neighbours for $5.00 each. "Why on earth would you do that?" said the clerk, "You buy them from me at $6.00 each?" To which the farmer replied, "I know, but it sure beats farming for a living."*

In a keynote presentation Marcia Steele, CSP, shared her experiences with her recent fight with Cancer. That created an uncomfortable tension in her audience, but Marcia Steele was not looking for sympathy. She was using a personal experience to make a point in her presentation. Yet she had to make that message palatable to that audience. When she talked about her experience with Chemotherapy and losing her hair, she discovered a surprising benefit in that she "found she had a pretty head". Delivered with a challenging grin, this blunted the edge of the tension in the audience. The tension was dispelled even further as she joked about her wig and how "when it's loose enough, you have room to hide your car keys".

But the whole message became infinitely palatable when she removed her wig entirely and finished her presentation "au natural".

Marcia displayed considerable courage in talking about her illness, but also in using humor to ensure we weren't just being sorry for her, but instead, understood the entire message she was offering.

To Entertain

In this context, the Speaker moves closer to the role of comedian where his or her main function is to get the audience laughing. In this context the differences in the roles of the Speaker and the Comedian become blurred.

At the end of a number of days of intensive training and development, many organisations call on the services of a Humorist to lighten the tension of the participants. It is considered particularly important to allow conference or training participants to unwind before they go home to their families. This ensures that they don't take home the inhibiting effects of tension that may have been created in the meeting.

> *Two cannibals were eating a comedian when one said to the other,*
> *"Does this taste funny to you?"*

To add humor to his presentations in the early part of his career when he was speaking primarily on the topic of Self-Esteem, Jack Canfield frequently used a pile of cartoons.

Sadly, I haven't seen him present since the enormous success of the Chicken Soup for the Soul books he co-authored with Mark Victor Hansen. Mark however, rarely uses cartoons, but has a wonderful sense of humor and has more fun with his audiences than most speakers I know.

Currently, computer projection slides have become the medium for the use of cartoons. Unfortunately it has also become a crutch for many speakers who use computer software to support their memory or even their self-confidence.

Little Johnnie volunteered at school one morning that God lived in his bathroom!
The teacher asked how he knew that,
Whereupon Johnnie said,
Every morning my Dad beats on the bathroom door, and says, "God are you still in there".

If you feel it's appropriate for you to use cartoons to support some of the points you make in your presentations, please remember that these cartoons are the intellectual property of the cartoonist and should only be used with their permission.

To Get Paid

There used to be an old joke among speakers that you only use humour if you want to get paid. While that is becoming less factual, there is still a glimmer of truth in it. Speakers who use humor in their presentations will always be more popular and will be asked to return much more frequently than those who don't. It is simply a matter of fact that these speakers are enjoyed more and tend to be much more effective than those who don't use humor.

> Two people visited both Ireland and Scotland on a vacation trip.
> On their return, they were arguing which whisky was stronger, Scotch or Irish
> One of them voted for Irish Whisky and reasoned that it must be true, because he and his wife downed a whole bottle of it one night,
> and the next morning, went to six o'clock Mass.
> The other demanded to know why that proved Irish Whisky was stronger.
> The first one explained,
> "You see, we're both Methodist."

*I won't say he has a superiority complex,
but he once wrote a book called,
The 10 Greatest People in History... and my Views
on the Other Nine*

*New Year's Eve is a night when we all sing
"Auld Lang Syne" from the heart,
which isn't easy,
as none of us knows what it means!*

*My wife wanted to go to Bermuda on vacation.
I wanted to go to Hawaii.
So we split the difference.
We stayed home.*

Humor is No Laughing Matter

7 Rules of Humour on the Platform

Many speakers don't use humor because they feel they simply "can't tell a joke". This is rarely true. Most people can tell a joke as long as they focus on the right type of joke to tell.

For example, many people have difficulties recounting a long story or the "Vignette" which we discussed on page 16, but most people can deliver a "One-liner" as we discussed on page 11. The "one-liner" is the kind of humor that can be delivered successfully by almost anyone.

While the ability to create and deliver humour is partly a gift, there is a very scientific and practical part to it which, if learned, allows most people to create more fun on the platform and also at home and at work.

1. Surprise them!

The funniest joke in the world is the one where the punch line is totally and completely unexpected. The surprise is frequently the main reason the joke is funny. The punch-line comes out of left field, totally unexpected from the way your thought pattern has been guided in the set-up of the joke.

> "Give a man a fish and he'll eat for a day.
> Teach him how to fish,
> and he'll sit in a boat and drink beer all day."

The humorous suprise is what makes the joke.

> Behavioural scientists tell us that the teen years
> are a time of rapid change.
> Between the ages of 12 and 20,
> a parent can age 30 years.

> When his Mum told Jimmy he had his shoes on the
> wrong feet,
> he complained bitterly,
> "but they're the only feet I've got!"

2. Let Them Laugh

Always be listening to your audience when you speak. This advice is particularly true when you're using humor. When you hit the punch-line, listen to the audience's reaction, and in particular, to the way the laughter is coming out. In smaller groups of up to 100 people, the laughter will come at you in one lump. Larger groups usually deliver the laughter in waves and this makes it slightly more difficult to gauge the timing of your next comment.

If you're presentation is building to an important climax and your audience is laughing, wait for it to start to die down before resuming your presentation. In other words, let them laugh..... but not too long. If you wait until everyone has laughed and quietened before starting again, you've gone to long and you'll feel (and hear) an uncomfortable pause.

Sometimes you may want that pause following a laugh. That would be when you're going to create a heavy emotional or tense moment. Under this condition, you can let the laughter die down completely and then, with an appropriate change of voice pitch and tone, make the serious pronouncement.

However if you want the presentation to continue to build, you must always resume your presentation as the laughter is dying. Don't wait for the audience to finish, and never start again while the laughter is still building. Remember that people like to laugh and we don't do it nearly enough, so if you're going to encourage them, you must also give them the time and the opportunity.

3. Advance the Topic

Unlike the comedian, the speaker is usually there to deliver a message, therefore any humor that is used should be there to assist in that endeavour. Humor is best used to help underscore a point that's being made.

> *A few years ago, our daughter, Lesley, was working in Florida.*
> *She returned home for a brief vacation with a video tape of her bunje jumping.*
> *That tape scared her mother and I out of our wits.*
> *We asked her never to do that again.*
> *She agreed, and some time later, returned to Florida.. Three weeks later, we received an envelope in the mail from her.*
> *On the reverse side of the envelope were written the words,*
> *"O.K., so you don't want me to go Bunje Jumping."*
> *Inside were three photographs of her Sky-Diving!*

Obviously, I use that story about my daughter to underscore a number of points such as "be careful what you ask for, you may get it", or "the importance of being very specific".

> On entering late to a presentation
> being given by a local congressman,
> I asked a gentleman who was leaving the room,
> "Has the Congressman started speaking yet?"
> "Yes" he's been speaking for half-an-hour."
> "What is he talking about?" I asked.
> "I don't know" said the gentleman,
> "He hasn't said yet."

Humor can also advance the topic by using it as a transition piece in moving you from one point to another, or even from one emotion to another.

4. Appropriate Use of Humour

It is worthwhile to remember that there are many individuals in this world who have no sense of humor. Don't worry about them, they will fight stress in their own way. Your presentation must not live or die on the reaction (or lack thereof!) of any single individual in your audience. Their response will often be the same regardless of the appropriateness of the humor being used.

When I was a young man (back in the olden days when the air was clean and sex was dirty!) there was no such thing as "Appropriate Humor". The recipient or audience fell into one of two categories; either they *had* a sense of humor or they *didn't*. Today we are much more sensitive to the opinions and outlooks of others (or ought to be!), and the term "Politically Correct" has come into the language.

To ensure you can safely survive any joke-telling session or presentation in which you use humor, the rule is not to tell a joke at the expense of a group to which you do not belong, whether it be ethnic, religious, gender or a career.

In other words, if you're not a Scotsman, don't tell a joke about a Scot. They know the best ones anyway. Similarly, Lawyers tell the best Lawyer jokes. Poles tell the best Polish jokes..... etc. etc. etc.

It is always safest to tell a joke at your own expense, in other words, what we would refer to as self-effacing humour. This is not the same thing as self-deprecating humour which can constitute a verbal attack on yourself, and you may be surprised at how many people will come to your defence *against you!*

In spite of our utmost attempts at sensitivity, we will always find someone who will be offended at something we say, even if we say it with the best intentions and all the love and respect we can muster.

A few years ago, I was to be introduced at an after-lunch session by a woman who told me during the meal that she had forgotten my introduction. I immediately handed her a copy of one I always carry for such an occasion. After a few moments she told me she couldn't possibly read this. As it turned out, her problem was that the introduction included the phrase, "Ladies and Gentlemen". She advised me rather haughtily that her female associates were not "Ladies" and should not be addressed in that fashion.

Without commenting any further, let's just accept the fact that there are days when you just can't win. But keep trying.

When we discuss appropriate humor, there is one area of diversity that tends to be ignored, and that is "Age". How many times have you witnessed a young salesman trying to connect with an elderly client by telling him or her a joke and it falls flat? When we're relating humor to people outside of our own generation, it's essential to remember that the different generations tend to laugh at different things. A younger person may fail to see the humor in the following story.

> At 85 years of age, George had been a bachelor all his life, but he told his cronies that he had finally decided to get married. Curious about why he would choose to marry this late in life, they asked him, "Is she young?".
> "Well," said George, "she's only 83."
> O.K. then said his friends, "Is she rich?".

> "No, she gets a social security cheque just like we do."
> "In that case why are you marrying her?"
> George explained, "She drives.... at night!.".

The use of humor must also be appropriate to the Speaker, or the individual who is delivering that humor. Sometimes the joke itself is acceptable, but not from a particular speaker.

The most glaring example is an audience of teenagers who, although they may enjoy slightly off-colour humor between themselves, would be absolutely horrified if it were told to them by a middle-aged speaker. The joke may be acceptable, but the speaker will not be.

This also applies to each of us on a personal level. If we're not comfortable delivering a line, then simply don't do it. The audience will detect your discomfort and will not respond appropriately.

Similarly, the event or the audience may not be the right place to share a particular piece of material. Some years ago, a good friend and past

Toastmasters International World Champion of Public Speaking, Arabella Benson, was practicing a particular presentation where she used the line,

*"if a job's worth doing,
it's worth doing wrong at first"*.

This was a line she had used many times and was meant to offer encouragement to try something even although you won't be perfect at the first try. A lot like the advice I'm offering you regarding your use of humour. Unfortunately, this line was not going to work in this instance because the event was an annual meeting of Emergency Room Nurses, who deal with Life and Death situations on a regular basis. The line was instantly removed from the presentation.!

5. Personalize Your Material

You'll notice in the earlier joke, we talked about "George" who is identified as an elderly bachelor. This personalizes the joke, if only just a little. It ranks far and away above a story that starts with,

"…. this old guy told his cronies……".

When you're telling a joke from the platform, the work is in the "set-up" to make it as believable as possible in order for the "punch-line" to provide as much surprise as can be achieved. This believability can be created by personalizing the set-up by telling the story about a yourself, a friend or a relative. Make the individual very personal to you and the audience will follow along with the set-up and enjoy the joke even more. This will work even better if the audience knows the individual to whom you are referring and the joke is on them.

Be very careful about using an audience member as the butt of a joke. This could cause a feeling of animosity to rise against you from the rest of the audience. The problem is that the audience may not be aware of the relationship between the speaker and that audience member, and from their own relationship with the other audience member, may feel the joke is inappropriate and spring to their defence.

This happened in an interesting extreme when I was speaking to a group of my peers most of whom knew me well. I used some self-effacing humor which I thought was funny as the butt of the joke was myself. This is usually a safe target. However, on this occasion, I obviously crossed a very fine line and the audience felt as though I was coming down on myself too heavily and didn't respond well to my attempt at poking fun on myself.

> "Humour is the highest form of communication, and the most difficult.
> It can also be the most dangerous."
> Doc Blakely

6. Punchline

If you're going to tell a joke.... tell a joke! Don't quit on it halfway through, or deliver the punchline in the wrong way.

There are two basic ways to deliver a punchline. One is the "throw-away" line where the punchline is said very casually as though it didn't matter. This is frequently used with a very short one-liner where the intention is to raise a smile, but not disturb the flow of the speaker's thought pattern. With a throw-away line you are rarely going for a belly laugh, but usually a slight easing of nervous tension.

The standard punch-line however, must be delivered with conviction and confidence in the full expectation of getting a major humorous response.

Some years ago, I was trying out some new material and had included an old, old joke which should have worked, but didn't. I asked a friend to give me some feedback and help me figure out why it didn't work.

After she listened to me deliver the material a few times, she said, "it's obvious, you're not committing to the line!". Apparently, I had been treating it as a throw-away line, and was not therefore getting the response I needed at that point in the presentation. Once I committed to it properly, the response was hale and hearty, exactly what I had planned for at that point in the material.

Another point of consideration about the punchline that we mentioned earlier is, if you're going to do the set-up anyway, why not find two or three laughs along the way.

Also, the arrangement of the punch-line can make a difference to the power of the joke. The best effect can be achieved if the dominant word in the punch-line is moved as closely as possible to the end of the sentence; ideally the last word.

In one of my presentations, I mention a quote from Earl Nightingale who once said, "You become what you think about most." I then question the validity of the quote by saying,

> "If that were totally true,
> I'd have been a girl by the time I was 17."

This usually got a bit of a laugh, but it was never a real knee-slapper. However, I changed it to;

> "If that were totally true,
> by the time I was 17, I'd have been a girl.".

The difference in response was enormous. This is a powerful example of the positioning of the dominant (or punch) word. When the punch word was buried in the middle of the line it had minimal effect. When moved to the very end of the line, the audience was held in suspense until the very last moment, thus increasing the surprise and it's ultimate effect.

7. Practice, Practice, Practice.

Very few people can tell a joke or deliver a funny line really well the first time they do it. Everyone needs to practice, even the professional comics.

At his best, Dick Van Dyke was indisputably one of the funniest men who ever appeared on television. The characters he portrayed never failed to provide extraordinary joy to his millions of viewers over the years. Yet few people were aware that he arranged the shooting schedule for the show to start on Wednesday and finish with the final performance in front of a live audience on Tuesday evenings. This was done for a reason. When the other cast members were relaxing at home with their families on the weekend, Dick Van Dyke was also at home, but he was working on his routines and lines for the show so that, when Tuesday evening rolled around, he was at the top of his form and could deliver that flawless performance we had all come to expect of him.

"How do you get to Carnegie Hall?
Practice, man, practice!"

Humor is No Laughing Matter

Cultivating Your Own Sense of Humor

Many people tell me, "Oh, it's easy for you, you're so good at telling jokes, but I just have no sense of humor." In fact, during a recent seminar, a woman said to me,

> *"My daughter keeps telling me*
> *I have no sense of humor,*
> *and I think she may be right!"*

Happily the second part of the comment was said in jest, because the woman knew she hadn't lost her sense of humor, but she also knew she didn't laugh as much as she had in earlier years.

I did remind her that Teenagers around the house will either drive away your sense of humor forever, or will force you into developing one really quickly for the sake of survival.

Question:
"Why did God ask Abraham to sacrifice his 12-year old son?"

Answer:
> "Because if he had been 13,
> it wouldn't have been a sacrifice!"

For those of you who are struggling for survival, or merely want to develop your sense of humor, let me share 6 ideas with you.

1. Adopt a humorous attitude.

Adopting a humorous attitude is frequently as simple as walking around with a smile on your face. I love doing this, it always makes people wonder what you've been up to!

Lighten up and have fun.

Don't be one of these people who seem to be proud tell everyone,

*"I'm a bear
until I get my first coffee in the morning."*

Let's understand something about these people...... nobody cares! but in spite of that they are still a negative influence in your life, and if you happen to live with them, tell them to snap out of it.

If you don't live with them, don't hang around them!

The vast majority of these poor folks, were raised by, or mixed with, people who said that all the time. They don't know why they do it, they just think it's a 'cool' thing to say. It isn't! It creates negative energy that can only be countered with humour. By this time we should all understand the glass of water and if it's half empty or half full.

An Optimist is a husband who thinks the argument with his wife is finished when she says, "Fine!"

A Pessimist is a man who gets a clean bill of health from his doctor, and then seeks a second opinion.

2. Look for the joy in all you do

Many of us spend a significant portion of our time at work in an office where we have the opportunity of keeping some personal items on display. Most have a photograph or two of their loved one(s) in a high profile position, with a view to help them feel good about themselves in a relatively stressful environment. This technique works very well and I have used it during part of my own career.

Another version of this is a friends photograph of her family which acts as a screen saver on her computer. This lady has a handsome husband and 4 good-looking sons, three of whom are less than 5 years old. They are posed elegantly in this photograph which appears before her every time she takes a rest from her work on her computer. It's one of these very typical photographs of a beautiful family we all put on display and which usually elicits an "awwwwwww" of appreciation from anyone who sees it. However, having met her family on a number of occasions, I can tell you that her guys have only ever looked that good on one occasion in their lives, and that was when that particular photograph was taken. While it is certainly a family to be proud of, I suggested to her that her spirits could be lifted more effectively by one (or more) of the many photographs of her sons that can make her laugh.

As none of us are laughing (or even smiling) as often as we ought to at work, we should take every opportunity to increase that frequency and bring a little more joy into our hearts on a daily basis.

I started some months ago when my daughter gave me a particular photograph that was taken of my 8 month old Grandson while he was in fully belly-laugh mode. All I have to do is look at that photograph and I can't help but smile. Sometimes I even laugh out loud at the sight and thought of this little boy enjoying life as much as he does. It's significant that this effect has been continuous during the 10 months that photograph has been on my desk, and shows no signs of abating.

The sight of that photograph brightens my day, reduces any stress that may be present and allows me to relax a little and become much more productive.

Find a photograph or a scrap of memorabilia that has a special and a joyful meaning for you, and place it somewhere it will bring you joy. Some years ago I remember driving with an associate to an appointment when I saw a scrap of paper glued to the dashboard of his car. The message on the paper read, "I love you tons, daddy" and was signed by his daughter. When he saw me reading it he smiled warmly and said, "It puts the rest of the world into perspective.".

Some years ago, a Toastmaster from Montreal, Canada was conducting a workshop on Self Esteem at a Regional Conference, when he gave everyone in his audience a small scrap of satin cloth to carry with them at all times. The idea was that they touch it frequently during the day to remind themselves how special they are to themselves and to the many people in their lives who loved them. I remember carrying that piece of cloth with me for a long, long time and, every time I found it in my jacket pocket, I smiled.

It doesn't take a lot to bring the joy of life into your world. Sometimes all we need, is to be reminded to do so.

"I love my job, it's the work I can't stand."

One idea I came across years ago was to appoint a Manager of Mirth in the workplace. For the most widespread effect, this should be a revolving position with everyone taking the position for at least one week. The main function of the job would be to provide at least one piece of humor or source of amusement every day for his or her co-workers.

In some places, this could be a cartoon on the Notice Board which should always be limited to one at a time in case it takes up too much space. Alternatively, there may be a budget for a series of poster size cartoons which can be purchased from a variety of sources.

Practical jokes that are directed against any particular member of the group must be avoided.

Perhaps the wearing of a ridiculous hat or other piece of clothing may work. Maybe a Loud Tie competition would work. After all, every man I know has at least one in his closet.

Let humor run rampant and every so often elect the

best Manager of Mirth and award a prize that would bring a smile to their face.

You might be amazed at how many in that dour group you call your co-workers, can actually reveal a previously unknown and wonderful sense of humor. All they were waiting for was permission to let it loose. Don't forget that a lot of workplaces tacitly discourage humor, so this might be a significant change in corporate attitudes.

3. Laugh at least 20 times a day

As we've said before, most adults average only 15 laughs per day which compares extremely unfavourably with 5 year-old children who laugh as much as 400 times per day. To improve your disposition (and therefore, those around you) I suggest you work at improving your frequency of mirthful moments.

If you're having a hard day at the office, think about something enjoyable outside the office. Take a part of your mind and move it outside and at least have fun mentally. You'll find that your mind can't tell the difference between you really having fun and the mental substitute.

You may even want to indulge in a song or two, but if the environment or the condition of your singing voice renders this unacceptable to your associates, just hum quietly to yourself. The trick is to choose a happy tune, or at least a type of music that gives you a good positive energy. For me, big band swing music or dixieland jazz will put a smile on my face a lot faster than anything else.

Continue to look for the joyous moments in your every day existence, in your surroundings and in the people around you. If you see one or two people laughing at the other end of the mall or the office, laugh with them, even if you don't know why.

The beauty of laughter is that it is infectious.

Watch a young child. If the adults around her start to laugh, she'll laugh too, even although she has no idea why. It also works with adults.

Try it, you'll like it!

4. Watch a funny movie, video or TV show at least once a week.

I may be dating myself, but one of my all time favourite TV shows has got to be "MASH". Here is true comedy on screen. Yet you'll notice that in almost every episode there was a touch of tragedy intermingled with the humor. The writers of "MASH" and the magnificent cast understood their role and their responsibility; to mix the two faces of tragedy and comedy.

"Who's Line is it Anyway" provides a full program of uncontrolled and impromptu comedy. This has got to be the most difficult type of humor to work with, and yet it is obvious from the cast of that show, that they have learned a craft which allows them to plumb the depths of their talent to bring out the humor in the various situations they're faced with.

It's often too easy to say, "Well, I could NEVER do THAT!". I would certainly agree that most of us could never do it that well, but I have seen it done in a party of non-professionals, and done surprisingly well. It simply proves that each of us has a little kid in us somewhere who still wants to get out and make a fool of themself. Or could it be, we all secretly (or sometimes not so secretly) love the attention, applause and laughter that a successful comedy routine can bring us, even more than the admiration we could earn from an excellent dramatic reading. The attention and applause may be the same.

The difference is the laughter.

We instinctively know that our spirits yearn for joy. So stop fighting it, go get it! Find it on TV. You may have to watch some of the reruns on cable or on a Video, but they're available.

Charlie Chaplin, Buster Keaton, Jerry Lewis, the Marx Brothers and the 3 Stooges are all still available on video. We all have our favourites. They are all still funny. Make a pact with yourself that you will consciously watch something really funny for at least one hour every week. You'll be amazed at the difference in your outlook and attitude.

5. Start a cartoon file

I believe that everyone should have a file of great cartoons that they've clipped from a newspaper or magazine. Leaf through it once in a while, or have your current favourite pinned up where you can enjoy it.

Any time I have to spend a few minutes in my Doctor's waiting room, I ransack his pile of magazines for one entitled "Stitches" which is published in Ontario, Canada. This is a medical magazine and, while I'm not in the medical field and don't understand most of the medical jokes, the cartoons in this magazine are some of the best you'll find anywhere.

When you start collecting your cartoons, don't hoard them. Share them with others. In fact if you want to raise the laughter level in the office or workplace, remove the punch line and challenge others to add theirs. Have a competition for the best punch line. In other words have fun with them

6. Exchange jokes with each other

O.K...... I know, you can't tell jokes, you get halfway through and forget the punchline! That's normal. Very few people can tell a joke properly the first time around. Every professional comedian, humorist and speaker practices telling jokes and stories until they find the best way. So don't worry about how good you are, just keep practicing.

A man was sitting at the traffic lights in his Rolls Royce when a little Skoda pulled up alongside and the driver signalled to the man to wind down his window so he could speak to him.
   "Nice car, do you have a telephone it?" he asked.
   "Of course I do." came the rather pompous reply.
   "Do you have a bed in there?"
   "No-one has a bed in their car."
   "Well, I do!" said the Skoda driver
as the lights changed and he drove off. That really annoyed the driver of the Rolls, because he was heavily into one-upmanship, and he couldn't bear anyone in a Skoda have something he didn't, so he investigated the matter with the Rolls Royce dealership.

"Certainly sir, we can put a bed in your car, what would you prefer, single, double, king-size or four-poster?"

In no time at all, he collected his Rolls with it's new bed and went out looking for the Skoda driver to prove to him that he was now as good as he was. Eventually he found the Skoda in a parking lot with the windows all steamed up. The Rolls driver knocked on the door as thre was obviously someone in there. When the driver opened the door to the Skoda, he was soaking wet and quite abruptly he asked,

"What do you want?"

I just wanted you to know I now have a bed in my car! said the Rolls driver rather proudly.

To which the Skoda driver said......

"For this you got me out of the shower?"

You may want to make a pact with a few friends to tell each other at least one joke every week. At first this may be difficult, but if you persist you'll find yourself having 2 or 3 jokes you want to share with these mirth seekers. Remember, these jokes are just for fun, there doesn't have to be a point to them.

When we speak about telling jokes, the internet doesn't count. A good joke has got to be shared verbally in order to make it work. As you might see from some of the examples in this book, reading a joke doesn't always do justice to it. Try repeating some of them out loud for a friend.

Conclusion

An Article in "Nations Business" a few years ago identified that one of the seven qualities of a great boss was a sense of humor. I suggest to you that one of the seven qualities of a great person is a sense of humor.

In today's society, we share many aspects of ourselves with others. We share our knowledge, our wisdom, our beliefs and our standards and we usually receive much more than we get. So it is with humor. Give it away and it will return to you in even greater abundance.

Laugh and the world laughs with you.
Cry and your mascara will run!

Humor is No Laughing Matter

Humor is No Laughing Matter

ANOTHER BOOK BY THE AUTHOR

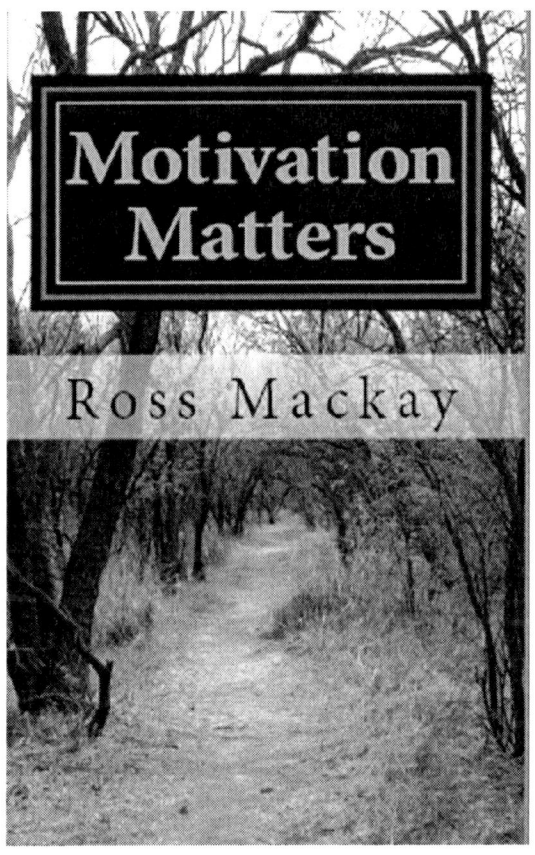

A treasury of quotes and thoughts to motivate you at work, and inspire you in life. In this book, I am privileged to share with you the ideas of selected experts on this human experience in an attempt to repay the immense value they have afforded me throughout my life.

available at:
www.rossmackay.com

Humor is No Laughing Matter